Communication Information

By
Linda Barr

Illustrated by
Ron Himler

Columbus, OH

The **McGraw·Hill** Companies

Photo Credits

53 ©CERN;
55 ©Sam Ogden/Photo Researchers, Inc.

MHEonline.com

 SRA

Imprint 2012

Copyright © 2005 by SRA/McGraw-Hill.

Send all inquiries to:
SRA/McGraw-Hill
8787 Orion Place
Columbus, OH 43240-4027

Printed in the United States.

ISBN 0-07-604478-5

10 DOC 14

Contents

Chapter 1
Plant Paper

Paper is becoming less and less necessary in our modern world. People used to send letters in the mail, but now many people send e-mails instead. Newspapers are still good places to find information, but more and more people are reading the news on Web sites. Businesses once used tons of paper, but now they do the same work on computers.

Yet computers sometimes crash, and files can be lost, destroyed, or inaccessible. Information on paper is safer.

Long ago, there was no paper. It hadn't been invented. People couldn't write the stories they heard or the things they learned; instead they had to remember everything. Imagine how hard that would be!

To record their ideas, people carved or painted pictures on cave walls, stone tablets, or other hard surfaces. However, carving in stone isn't easy, and people couldn't carry these pictures with them if they had to leave the area.

The ancient Egyptians solved this problem by making papyrus from plants. Papyrus is flat and lightweight, so it's easy to write on and carry. To make papyrus, the Egyptians sliced plant stems into strips and pasted together the strips. Then they stacked three layers of strips, soaked them in water, pressed them, and let them dry.

The word *paper* comes from *papyrus,* but papyrus isn't really paper. Papyrus is made up of stems pasted together. If you look at papyrus closely, you might see the stems.

A man from China named Ts'ai Lun invented paper similar to what we use today. About 1,900 years ago, he cut bamboo and tree bark, mixed them with water, and pounded them into a soft mush, or pulp.

Ts'ai spread the pulp, let it dry, and pressed it into a flat, smooth sheet. This paper was possible to make and easy to carry. In time, people around the world learned how to make paper. They tried using different plants, such as straw, silk, and seaweed. Some of these plants were more dependable than others.

The Chinese didn't only write on paper. They were the first to use paper as money, and they also used paper to make windows, umbrellas, toys, and many other things.

You can make paper in almost the same way Ts'ai did. Ask an adult to help you follow the steps on the next two pages.

How to Make Paper

To make a screen, bend a coat hanger into a square, and slide it into old panty hose.

Tear two newspaper pages into pieces. Half fill a blender with warm water and some of the paper, then close the lid, and have a responsible adult turn on the blender. Continue to add water and the rest of the paper to make a thick pulp.

Plug a sink, pour in the pulp, and mix in two tablespoons of white glue.

Slide the screen under the pulp, and slowly lift it, letting the water drain through.

Spread the pulp in an even layer on the screen, let it dry, and then carefully peel it off. Ask an adult to iron the dried pulp so it's flat. You have made paper!

Chapter 2
The Pony Express

If you wrote a letter on paper to someone today and sent it in the mail, it would probably take a day or two to get to its destination. But in the early 1800s there was no convenient way to carry mail across the United States, and delivery time for mail was weeks or sometimes months. Why did the mail system take so long?

The United States was not as populated then as it is now. There were vast, nearly inaccessible areas with no roads and no easy way to get from place to place. Stagecoaches and trains were used on roads and train tracks, and steamboats were used where there were no roads. Mail carriers often had to go long distances out of their way to deliver the mail.

When gold was discovered in California in 1848, pioneers began moving farther west. Getting mail from the East to the West and back again was difficult, and many Californians began to feel isolated from the rest of the world. Mail was delivered to California one of two ways. The first was by stagecoach, which was supposed to take twenty-four days, but instead it often took months.

The second option was to put mail on a ship that sailed south around the United States to Panama, then put it onto a train that crossed Panama, and then put it onto another ship the rest of the way to the West Coast. This process could also take a month or more. A more feasible solution was needed, and William Russell was the man who thought of it.

In 1860 Russell came up with the idea to put people on horses and send them across the country to deliver mail. Many people thought this was impossible because of bad weather conditions year-round, but Russell persisted. The Pony Express's first trip began on April 3, 1860, in Missouri, and arrived in California just ten days later.

One rider would ride his horse for ten or fifteen miles and then would change horses at a station to continue his journey. He would travel between seventy-five and one hundred miles in one day before another rider would take his place to continue across the country. Pony Express riders had to travel 1,800 miles from Missouri to California.

The mail was carried in saddlebags riders carried as they rode. Riders could weigh no more than 125 pounds, because the filled saddlebag weighed 40 pounds, and the horse could carry only 165 pounds total.

The Pony Express stayed in operation a little more than a year. It was discontinued in 1861 when the next great communication invention—the telegraph—was created.

Chapter 3
Dots and Dashes

The invention of the telegraph drastically changed the United States mail system. No one at that time had phones or computers, and a handwritten letter could take weeks to be delivered, even if it was carried by the Pony Express.

Imagine that you live in New York City in 1837, the time before the Pony Express. You send a letter to your cousin in San Francisco, with whom you have a close friendship.

Your letter will travel by train and stagecoach. The trip is very long— it might take months. If your cousin writes back, you won't receive the letter for a very long time.

This method of mail delivery was something people had to live with in the early 1800s. But a great change was on the way. The same year this old delivery system was still being used, Samuel Morse invented the telegraph, which sends an electric signal over a wire.

Morse's telegraph system works like this: Holding down the telegraph key a short time sends a dot. Holding down the key longer sends a dash. Morse wrote a code of dots and dashes; for example, "dot-dash" means the letter A. A telegraph operator uses this code to spell words.

In 1838 Morse demonstrated to people how his code worked, but few people cared. They didn't understand how useful it could be.

Six years later the first telegraph line was laid from Washington, D.C., to Baltimore, Maryland—a distance of only forty miles. Morse sent the first message over the new line using his code. This time people noticed. Morse code could change their lives! For the first time it was possible to send messages that would arrive the same day. People loved the idea.

More telegraph lines were laid, mostly along railroad tracks. Railroad stations sent telegraphs to one another to communicate when trains arrived and left.

Soon people in the towns near the railroad tracks began to use the lines. These people had been isolated from many of their loved ones before, but now they could easily communicate with friends and family who lived far away.

Citizens in the towns far from railroad tracks soon wanted to send telegraphs also. This meant new stations had to be built in order to reach these faraway towns. Additional, brand-new towns began to pop up near the newly built stations because people wanted to live near the telegraph.

Soon people in Europe wanted to send telegraphs too. In 1847 the first telegraph line was laid in Europe. Many more lines followed.

Sending a telegraph was actually quite easy. You went to the station, an operator typed your message in Morse code, and off your message went.

The long-awaited first transcontinental telegraph line was laid in 1861, finally connecting the East and West and eliminating the need for the Pony Express. When the telephone was invented in 1876, Morse code and the telegraph fell into the background as well.

Chapter 4
A Signal to the World

Martha Coston was destined for leadership. She was born in 1826. When she grew up, she helped invent a system of communication that would eventually aid the United States Navy. During a time when few women worked outside the home, Coston was working hard at developing her invention.

Coston's husband, Benjamin, was also an inventor. Sadly, he died when she was just twenty-one years old. One day Coston found some drawings her husband had been working on, and she realized he had been designing an idea for a new signal light called a flare. He thought if ships were in trouble or needed to communicate, the ships could use this flare to signal one another or to signal people onshore.

This took place long before computers or telephones were invented, but some ships were starting to use Morse code. Before he died, Coston's husband had been ready to test his new light. Coston decided to continue her husband's work and to carry out the test in his memory. Coston convinced the navy to test the flare her husband had developed. Unfortunately, the navy was unimpressed. They did not see a need for the flare.

Instead of giving up, Coston hired some men to help her experiment with the light. Coston and her workers experimented for ten years. She wanted to have red, white, and blue lights, each with a different meaning, but she and her workers were able to make only red and white lights.

Then one day Coston happened to see some fireworks with blue lights.

Coston wrote to the man who had made the fireworks. He couldn't help her create a blue light that was bright enough, but he did send the materials to make a green one. As a result, Coston was able to create three colors for her signal—red, white, and green.

In 1859 Coston got a patent for her lights. She put the patent in her husband's name.

Now that the lights worked reliably, the navy wanted to buy some to help its military ships signal one another. Coston set up a company to manufacture her ship signals. She also got a patent for her signals in several countries in Europe. Many European countries bought the patent from her so they could make their own lights.

After the Civil War began, the navy wanted to manufacture its own lights, so it bought Coston's patent for $20,000. However, it ended up costing the navy more to manufacture the lights on its own than to buy the lights from Coston. The navy decided to form a partnership with Coston and continue buying the lights from her. Yet Coston didn't get rich. To help her country, she charged the navy only for the cost of supplies.

When the war ended, the navy owed Coston $120,000, but they paid her only $15,000. Regardless, Coston's lights had helped win battles and save lives.

Coston's two sons eventually took over her company, which manufactured signal lights for one hundred years. Some ships at sea still use her lights.

Chapter 5
The Code Talkers

During World War II, the United States and Japan were enemies. When the American Marines sent secret messages to their military troops, they didn't want the Japanese to be able to read them.

Some people thought about using the language of the Native American Navajo as a secret code. The Navajo language isn't written; Navajo learn it by listening and memorizing. At that time, few other people knew the Navajo language.

Some Navajo showed the marines how the code could work. A marine would write a message in English, and then a Navajo would read the message and say the words in his own language. Another Navajo listened to the Navajo words and repeated the message in English.

Machines could send codes, but they took thirty minutes to relay the code. Besides, the Japanese were able to decipher most of the machines' codes.

The marines decided to use the Navajo code, and twenty-nine Navajo began training as code talkers. They made up an even harder code. Let's say a code talker said four Navajo words that mean "sheep," "tooth," "owl," and "pig." Then another code talker used the first letter of each of these words to spell another English word.

Can you figure out the word?

The code talkers also made up new meanings for Navajo words. For example, *besh-lo* means "iron fish" in Navajo, but the code talkers used *besh-lo* to mean "submarine." *Lo-tso* means "whale" in Navajo, but the code word *lo-tso* meant "battleship." *Dah-he-tih-hi* means "hummingbird," but in the code it meant "fighter plane."

The code talkers were sent to battlegrounds near Japan. There they helped send secret messages to American troops. Some messages told troops which way to go, while others warned that the enemy was moving in or of other dangers. In this way, the code talkers helped the marines win battles and saved many American lives.

In one battle, six code talkers worked for two days straight. They sent eight hundred messages without one mistake.

The Japanese heard the code talkers sending some of their messages. They had been able to break many codes, but not this one!

More than four hundred Navajo worked as code talkers, but their part in the war was kept secret.

The code was also used in the Korean War and the Vietnam War. No one explained how it worked until 1968, and now we know all about code talkers. We've learned how creative and brave they were. The code talkers have been given medals and awards for their service. They helped keep American soldiers safe and America's people free. They were true defenders of freedom!

Chapter 6
Amazing Grace

You've probably never heard of Grace Hopper, but she changed the world. Without Hopper, computers might not be as helpful as they are today.

Hopper was born in 1906. Airplanes had just been invented, and the first cars were being built. No one had even imagined computers.

Hopper studied math in college. Back then, few women went to college, and even fewer studied math, but Hopper was one of a kind.

Hopper became a college teacher and later joined the navy. There she started working with a computer—one of the first in the world.

This computer, called Mark I, wasn't at all like computers today. Mark I weighed five tons and was fifty-five feet long! With 760,000 parts combined, it was one of a kind, just like Hopper.

To make the computer work, Hopper punched holes in a strip of paper and sent the strip through the computer. The pattern of the holes commanded the computer, giving it specific tasks to do.

Mark I could do some mathematical problems, but it could store only seventy-two words at one time. How many words do you think a computer can store today? Billions!

When the first computers broke down, Hopper helped fix them. Once when she found a moth in one computer, she said the computer "had a bug." Since then, computer problems of any sort have been called bugs.

Hopper not only named computer bugs but also created a language called COBOL. COBOL controls computers with words, not numbers. Hopper designed ways for computers to communicate in words.

Some people thought COBOL couldn't work, but Hopper proved otherwise. She illustrated how companies could use COBOL. For example, COBOL could help companies send bills to customers. COBOL made computers more useful to the average person.

Before COBOL, a person had to know a lot of math to use a computer. Now people just have to know words to use a computer.

In 1966 Hopper retired from the navy at age sixty. She had helped make computers much smaller, more powerful, and more common. The next year the navy asked Hopper to work on a small project—and she worked for nineteen more years! During that time she became the first woman admiral, which is one of the top ranks a person can be in the navy. After those nineteen years Hopper retired again for good. She had earned it.

Hopper died in 1992. She had received many awards over her lifetime, but she received no patents, because there were no patents in the computer field at that time. Today there are millions of computer patents.

Hopper's intelligent work made it easier to use computers, changing our lives. She was truly amazing.

Chapter 7
Caught in the Web

While Grace Hopper was making computers easier to use, others were inventing the Internet. By 1983 the Internet was in use. The Internet links computers all over the world, creating a network of computers. It lets people send and receive files and e-mails as well as search for information. But in 1983 it wasn't easy to find information on the Internet.

Today when we want information on something from a computer, we enter the topic into a search engine and pages on the topic come up. Back then there was no way to do a search. You had to enter the name or address of each and every file you wanted. If you didn't know the name, you were out of luck. Using a computer to get information wasn't very easy or much fun!

Tim Berners-Lee made the Internet more useful and more fun. Berners-Lee was born in England in 1955. In 1980 he was working for a company that owned many computers. It was hard for everyone in the company to share files. Berners-Lee solved that problem by figuring out how to connect information together. This was the beginning of the World Wide Web.

As part of the Web, Berners-Lee invented two languages, HTML and HTTP. Have you seen those letters before? HTML names the pages on the Web. HTTP allows the Web to send the pages from computer to computer.

Berners-Lee invented a browser to help people find these Web pages. Two browsers we use today are Internet Explorer and Netscape. These browsers allow us to "surf the Web."

Many Web sites have information on the same topic, and some sites are linked to others with similar information. To allow people to jump from one site to another, Berners-Lee used hypertext—usually one or more words displayed in blue or black and underlined. If you click on hypertext, the computer will jump to another Web site. It's quick and easy!

In 1991 Berners-Lee put the first Web site on the Internet. Now millions of people around the world use the World Wide Web every day to send mail, get information, do business, shop, have fun, and experience the world.

Before the Internet was developed, daily life was much different. For instance, when students had to do research to write papers for school, they went to the library and found books to help with their research. Today it's still important to read books, but the Internet has nearly as much useful information and is easier to get.

Berners-Lee's invention has made millions of lives easier. You might think he must be incredibly rich. Although Berners-Lee has received many awards, he has received no money. He invented the Web for free and holds no patents on it. He wanted everyone to be able to use it freely. Now Berners-Lee is looking for ways to make the Web even more useful.

Robert Mora / Alamy

Chapter 8
Smiling Robots

Do you think a robot can feel happy or sad? Can it understand how you are feeling? Believe it or not, Cynthia Breazeal is building robots that act like they have feelings. Breazeal's first robots were just heads with many moving parts. If you spoke kindly to one, it would smile; if you yelled, the robot would bow its head sadly.

Breazeal worked with a company in Hollywood to make her latest interesting robot, named Leonardo. Leonardo is two and one-half feet tall and furry. He is not designed to walk; instead he has a "smart" brain. Inside Leonardo are sixty small motors; thirty of these make Leonardo's face move.

Breazeal is programming Leonardo to "understand," or interpret, how people feel. You can recognize how people feel by looking at their faces, right? Soon Leonardo will be able to do that too. Leonardo can already understand directions and carry them out. For example, if you tell him to push a button, he will. When you point, he looks where you're pointing.

Soon Leonardo will be able to know from your frown that he has made a mistake. If Leonardo doesn't understand you, he will look confused so you know you must repeat your instructions. In these ways, Leonardo will communicate with people and build relationships by copying and interpreting human emotions.

Of course, not all robots are like Leonardo. Some do basic jobs such as painting car doors in a factory twenty-four hours a day. Other robots do very dangerous jobs such as going into buildings to find bombs.

These robots can do only one job. They cannot learn a new job or understand what people tell them, but Leonardo can.

Breazeal's robots are designed to interact with people and learn from them. These robots are much more "humanish" than other robots. Because of this, Breazeal's new robots have many potential uses, such as helping people who can't move around easily. The person could tell the robot, "Please bring me a glass of water," and off the robot would go!

These robots could also help people who have difficulty speaking and therefore are unable to tell the robots what they need. To ask for help, these people could instead use hand signals the robot would understand. If a person felt sad, the robot would interpret the person's expression and understand that too.

Breazeal's robots are taking communication in a new, exciting direction. What do you think other future robots might be like?